The Blue Room

Freely Adapted from
Arthur Schnitzler's *La Ronde*

by **David Hare**

FOUNDED 1830

New York Hollywood London Toronto
SAMUELFRENCH.COM

IMPORTANT BILLING AND CREDIT REQUIREMENTS

All producers of THE BLUE ROOM *must* give credit to the Author of the Play in all programs distributed in connection with performances of the Play and in all instances in which the title of the Play appears for purposes of advertising, publicizing or otherwise exploiting the Play and/or a production. The name of the Author *must* also appear on a separate line, on which no other name appears, immediately following the title, and *must* appear in size of type not less than fifty percent the size of the title type.

CORT THEATRE

Ⓢ A Shubert Organization Theatre

Gerald Schoenfeld, *Chairman*   **Philip J. Smith,** *President*

Robert E. Wankel, *Executive Vice President*

THE SHUBERT ORGANIZATION   SCOTT RUDIN   ROBERT FOX   ROGER BERLIND   ABC, INC.

PRESENT

NICOLE KIDMAN · IAIN GLEN

IN THE DONMAR WAREHOUSE PRODUCTION OF

THE BLUE ROOM

FREELY ADAPTED FROM ARTHUR SCHNITZLER'S LA RONDE
BY DAVID HARE

DESIGNED BY
MARK THOMPSON

LIGHTING BY
HUGH VANSTONE

ORIGINAL MUSIC BY
PADDY CUNNEEN

SOUND BY
SCOTT MYERS

GENERAL MANAGEMENT
STUART THOMPSON

TECHNICAL
SUPERVISOR
GENE O'DONOVAN

PRODUCTION
STAGE MANAGER
DAVID HYSLOP

PRESS REPRESENTATIVE
BONEAU/BRYAN–BROWN

DIRECTED BY
SAM MENDES

CHARACTERS

The girl	(Irene)
The cab driver	(Fred)
The au pair	(Marie)
The student	(Anton)
The married woman	(Emma)
The politician	(Charlie)
The model	(Kelly)
The playwright	(Robert)
The actress	
The aristocrat	(Malcolm)

Schnitzler's *Reigen* was said by its author to be 'completely unprintable' and was therefore distributed only 'to be read among friends' in 1900. Its eventual premiere was closed down by the police in Vienna in 1921, and the actors in its first Berlin production the same year had to endure a six-day trial on charges of obscenity.

In 1950 Max Ophuls made his famous film, starring among others, Gerard Philipe, Danielle Darrieux, Jean-Louis Barrault and Simone Signoret. Ophuls adapted the text with extreme freedom, and introduced the figure — not in Schnitzler — of the all-seeing ringmaster, played by Anton Walbrook. ("What am I in the story? I am in short any of you. I am the incarnation of your desire to know everything.") Since the success of that film, the play is better known as *La Ronde*.

The Blue Room is written to be performed with only two actors playing all the parts. It is set in one of the great cities of the world, in the present day.

Literal translation by Julian Hammond

1. THE GIRL AND THE CAB DRIVER

(Darkness. Music. You have the impression of the stage opening up, as if it were expanding. You begin to see a GIRL, sitting on a bench, smoking a cigarette. As the stage grows around her, it becomes clear she is under a scrubby tree by the side of a street. She looks 18, like an amateur, in a short black leather skirt and shoes, but she also has an odd self-confidence. A CAB DRIVER walks past. The girl lifts her arm.)

GIRL. Hey. *(The CAB DRIVER stops. A silence.)* What? What did you say?

CAB DRIVER. I didn't say anything.

GIRL. I thought you said something.

CAB DRIVER. No.

GIRL. What made me think you just spoke? *(She puts out her cigarette.)* Do you want to come home with me?

CAB DRIVER. Do I want to go home with you? Go *home*? Why would I want to go home with you? *(She is impassive, not responding.)* Where is your home?

GIRL. Quite near.

CAB DRIVER. Where?

GIRL. South.

CAB DRIVER. I'm not going south.

GIRL. We can take a taxi.

CAB DRIVER. *Take* a taxi. I drive a fucking taxi.

GIRL. Is it yours?

CAB DRIVER. It's mine.

GIRL. I mean, does it belong to you? *(He turns to go.)* So?

CAB DRIVER. I haven't got any money. I just spent the lot on sushi.

GIRL. So?

(The CAB DRIVER looks at her a moment.)

CAB DRIVER. Right, I've heard about you, you're new. Aren't you?

GIRL. New-ish.

CAB DRIVER. How long?

GIRL. A week.

CAB DRIVER. You enjoying it?

GIRL. Once or twice.

(He looks at her, tempted.)

CAB DRIVER. How far is this place of yours?

GIRL. It's ten minutes by cab.

CAB DRIVER. Oh look, forget it. Ten minutes? No. Forget it. I have to work. I've made nothing tonight. And I'm not doing it in the car. It's the first rule of driving. I never do it in the car.

GIRL. Give me a kiss.

CAB DRIVER. Here?

(She takes his hand and leads him quickly to a darker place across the street.)

GIRL. Now give me a kiss. *(She kisses him. It's magical, suspended for a moment. They stay in each others' arms. It is dark in the street and deserted.)* The kiss is the best bit. I like the kiss best.

CAB DRIVER. It's still too far.

(He looks at her. They start to walk towards the river. As they go down by the riverside, it is very beautiful, the reflection of the water thrown high against the wall.)

GIRL. What do you think? Do you think you'll always want to drive a cab?

CAB DRIVER. Shall we just stick to what we're doing?

(She throws a glance at him.)

GIRL. What I want … what I really need is someone long-term.

I need someone ambitious.

 CAB DRIVER. Long-term I'd make you jealous.

 GIRL. Oh yeah?

 CAB DRIVER. Sure.

 GIRL. Why?

 CAB DRIVER. I'm irresistible. Women can't resist me.

 GIRL. Watch out. It's dark down here. One foot wrong and you're in the river.

 CAB DRIVER. I'd love to be in the river.

(She smiles. He tries to push her up against the wall.)

 GIRL. Let's do it on the bench. There's one over there.

 CAB DRIVER. Let's do it here.

 GIRL. Watch out, or we'll both be in the water ...

 CAB DRIVER. Great ...

 GIRL. We'll both be in the water.

(Music engulfs them. The lights go out. A projected slide reads: THREE MINUTES.)

• • • • •

(Light returns. The GIRL is lying on the ground. The CAB DRIVER is kneeling beside her, his hands on his knees.)

 GIRL. It would have been better on the bench.

 CAB DRIVER. On the bench. Off the bench. Up the fucking wall. What's the difference? Up you get.

 GIRL. Hey, where you going?

 CAB DRIVER. Back to work. *(Suddenly he reaches down with unexpected tenderness and pulls her up. He smiles.)* I told you. I've done no business tonight.

(He begins to leave.)

 GIRL. What's your name?

 CAB DRIVER. Oh no, I'm not telling you my name.

 GIRL. My name's Irene.

CAB DRIVER. Irene, well!

GIRL. What's yours? *(They both smile. He turns to go.)* Hey listen ...

CAB DRIVER. What?

GIRL. Come on.

CAB DRIVER. What? What are you asking?

GIRL. Come on. I didn't want any money. Really. I didn't. But, please: give me some money.

(He looks at her a moment.)

CAB DRIVER. It went on the sushi. I'm not an idiot, Irene.

(He goes.)

GIRL. I'll be here tomorrow.

2. THE CAB DRIVER AND THE AU PAIR

(At once the sound of Elvis Presley. A slow ballad is being amplified very loudly and resonantly inside a neon-lit dance hall. Suddenly a door opens. Warm colored light falls across a darkened space, and onto the CAB DRIVER and the AU PAIR as they come on a wave of good humor into a darkened storeroom, next to a dance hall. She is young, with a foreign accent and wearing a dress which is subtly too small for her.)

CAB DRIVER. Show me. Go on. Show me again.
AU PAIR. You won't get it.
CAB DRIVER. I will get it. You wait. I will get it.

(Move by move, she demonstrates an intricate jive maneuver. She does it beautifully. He copies, learning.)

AU PAIR. I do that.
CAB DRIVER. Uh-huh.
AU PAIR. I do that. Then I do that.

(He gets it. They laugh together at the neatness of it.)

CAB DRIVER. It's great.
AU PAIR. By the way, what are we doing in here.
CAB DRIVER. Escaping the dance.

(He laughs and goes to the door.)

AU PAIR. Do you know my name? Can you even my name remember?
CAB DRIVER. Can I your name what? Go on, then, tell me. If it's so important.
AU PAIR. Marie. And you?

CAB DRIVER. Fred.
AU PAIR. I can't call you Fred.
CAB DRIVER. Why not?

(He closes the door. Pitch dark. She is wary.)

AU PAIR. It's so dark. My God, look how dark it is.
CAB DRIVER. Girls say they're scared, but what are they scared of?
AU PAIR. The dark. They're scared of the dark.

(He lights a match and makes a big arc with it.)

CAB DRIVER. This way, my dear. *(She smiles, slightly charmed. He lights a cigarette with the match, then pulls at a string above his head. A bare light bulb comes on. We are in a dusty store-room. Cardboard boxes, not much else.)* Why not tonight? Just tell me, why not?
AU PAIR. Because.
CAB DRIVER. Girls all say "because." I don't know what "because" means.
AU PAIR. It means because.
CAB DRIVER. Because it's Tuesday? Because we've only just met?
AU PAIR. Just because.
CAB DRIVER. Because you don't fancy me? It's hardly likely, is it?
AU PAIR. Why not?
CAB DRIVER. Well, just look at me.
AU PAIR. It's so dark I can't see you.
CAB DRIVER. So it can't be that, then, can it? *(She looks away, not responding.)* What's the problem? I promise you, I won't tell anyone.
AU PAIR. Oh, that's great. That's a real come-on …
CAB DRIVER. What's wrong with that?
AU PAIR. That makes me feel really sexy. What a great line! "I won't tell anyone"!

CAB DRIVER. Well, no-one'll know. *(She throws a sideways glance at him.)* So do you want to go back?

AU PAIR. Not yet.

(It's a concession. He cheers up.)

CAB DRIVER. Girls all say no.

AU PAIR. Girls do?

CAB DRIVER. I mean I'm not saying ...

AU PAIR. All girls say that?

CAB DRIVER. I'm not saying ... I'm not saying you're just any old girl. But the way I can tell you're a girl is because you say no.

AU PAIR. What do you think the reason is?

CAB DRIVER. I don't know.

AU PAIR. Why do you think I say no?

CAB DRIVER. Tell.

(She looks at him a moment.)

AU PAIR. Because of the risk. That's why. Why should I risk? That's the reason. It's not safe anymore. I'll only risk if ...

CAB DRIVER. If what?

AU PAIR. If it means something. If I'm to risk, it has to mean something. *(He takes her in his arms and they kiss. But she pulls away.)* So?

(The CAB DRIVER doesn't reply for a moment or two.)

CAB DRIVER. It means something. I promise.

AU PAIR. Does it? Does it really mean something? *(They go down together on a bed of cardboard, which crushes beneath them. He pulls again at the light string.)* I can't see your face.

CAB DRIVER. What's my face got to do with it?

AU PAIR. Let me see your face.

(She takes his face between her hands. Music engulfs them. Darkness. The projected slide reads: NINE MINUTES.)

• • • • •

(Near dark. A streak of ambient light hits only the CAB DRIVER. The two of them are still where they were.)

CAB DRIVER. Well there we are. *(He seems content.)* We can't lie on boxes all night. *(He lights a match for a cigarette, which they share.)* It's worth doing. Don't you think? For the cigarette. It's worth doing for the cigarette alone.

(The AU PAIR stretches.)

AU PAIR. Oh God.
CAB DRIVER. Oh God, what?
AU PAIR. Tu es un animal.
CAB DRIVER. That's right.

(She turns and looks at him.)

AU PAIR. Fred ...
CAB DRIVER. What? What, Fred?
AU PAIR. Tell me ... Tell me what you feel.
CAB DRIVER. What I feel?
AU PAIR. Yes.
CAB DRIVER. I've just shown you what I feel.

(There is a pause.)

AU PAIR. Frederick, tell me. Put into words.
CAB DRIVER. You know what I feel.
AU PAIR. Then kiss me.

(He stops and kisses her. The sound of Elvis grows again in the distance. It's romantic. Then he breaks.)

CAB DRIVER. I mean, I don't know. Feel's a big word. *(He gets up and pulls at the light string. She is looking at him from the floor. Then he pulls her up to her feet. She stands, adjusting her clothing.)* What are we going to do? Are we going back to the dance?

AU PAIR. If you like.

CAB DRIVER. I don't know. I'd like to go back but I'm sort of confused. To be honest, you've sort of confused me.

AU PAIR. Have I? How did I do that?

CAB DRIVER. I don't know. If I knew, then I wouldn't be confused. I knew where I was, now I don't. I don't like that. I don't like the feeling.

AU PAIR. No? *(He takes a step away.)* Well, I have to go.

CAB DRIVER. What.

AU PAIR. Yes. I have to get back. I'm treated like a servant. By the whole family. I have the cats to feed, the dogs, the humans. I'm a slave.

(The CAB DRIVER frowns, lost.)

CAB DRIVER. How are you going to get home?

AU PAIR. I'll walk.

CAB DRIVER. You can't walk. It's dangerous. At this time of night. Don't you want a lift. *(She doesn't answer. He raises his voice.)* I don't get it. What am I meant to say? What do you want me to say? I'm offering you a fucking lift. *(She smiles, and makes to go. He follows her, better-humored.)* And what does that mean? What does the smile mean? *(She smiles at him again.)* I'd like a dance. Can we have one more dance, please? I mean, if we don't, isn't it just a bit brutal?

(She looks at him.)

AU PAIR. Yes, Fred.

(The sound of the music grows. The CAB DRIVER closes his eyes and starts moving his hips.)

CAB DRIVER. You've taught me something. You've taught me something tonight. *(He points toward the lone chair in the room.)* Look, sit down. I'll get us a beer. We can dance in here.

AU PAIR. I don't have long.

CAB DRIVER. I won't be long. *(He opens the door. The crowded room glows with color and warmth.)* Don't you go now.

AU PAIR. I won't.

CAB DRIVER. Well, don't.

(He turns uncertainly and goes into the dance hall. The AU PAIR sits alone.)

3. THE AU PAIR AND THE STUDENT

*(The kitchen of a modern house in a well-off area of town. It is mod-
ishly decorated with stainless steel hooks from which hang a
faultless batterie de cuisine. There are gray venetian blinds on
the gleaming windows. At a big butchers' block table in the center of the room the AU PAIR is sitting in a blue blouse and
slacks and stunning blue slippers writing a letter. It is plainly
very hot. After a few moments the STUDENT appears at the
kitchen door. He has a book in his hand. He is in fashionable
jeans and a T-shirt. He is extremely nervous.)*

STUDENT. What are you doing?
AU PAIR. Writing a letter.
STUDENT. I see. Who to?
AU PAIR. A man I met at a dance.

(The STUDENT does not move.)

STUDENT. It's so hot. It's so unbelievably hot. It's never this
hot at this time of year. There's nobody left in town. Am I the only
person still working? They didn't take you to the country?
AU PAIR. No.

(She has stopped writing, but has not moved from the table.)

STUDENT. What's coolest? Vodka? Do we have vodka?
AU PAIR. We ran out. Your father drank the lot.
STUDENT. It's him insisted I read law. It's a family tradition.
AU PAIR. The drinking?
STUDENT. The law. *(He does not acknowledge the joke.)* It's
all right. I'll just have some water.
AU PAIR. There's the tap.
STUDENT. Can you get me a glass? *(It is clear he expects her*

to do it for him. She gets up, gets a glass from the cupboard, then goes to the tap, and turns it on. They are both running with sweat.) Let the water run, so it's really cool. *(The water overflows from the glass into the sink. She keeps it running.)* Who called?

AU PAIR. I'm sorry?

STUDENT. I heard the bell ring.

AU PAIR. Did you? When?

STUDENT. Earlier.

AU PAIR. When?

STUDENT. This morning. I've been up there so long I lose all track of time. I was expecting a friend.

AU PAIR. No friend. Here.

(She has taken the glass across to him and put it in his hand. He panics.)

STUDENT. I'll take it upstairs.

(He goes out. She goes to the mirror and adjusts her clothing, improving the line of her breasts against the shirt. She pours herself a glass of water. Before she can turn, the phone rings. She answers it.)

AU PAIR. Yes? You want another one? *(There is a slight pause.)* No. You come down.

(She drinks her own glass of water. Then gets a third glass from the cupboard and pours a fresh glass. As she finishes, he appears at the door, without a book.)

STUDENT. Thank you. So, excellent. You're enjoying it here? You get on with my father?

AU PAIR. Very well.

STUDENT. My mother likes you. You relate to my mother. Which is always important. I've found.

AU PAIR. Here.

STUDENT. She's an interesting woman, don't you think?

AU PAIR. Who?

STUDENT. My mother. *(She hands him a fresh glass and their hands touch once more.)* Thank you. *(He takes it and she moves away.)* Do we do things differently here? *(She doesn't answer.)* Come here, Marie.

AU PAIR. Sir.

STUDENT. Not sir. Nobody's called sir anymore. God. I hate that idea. Those days are gone.

AU PAIR. Sir?

(She has moved closer to him.)

STUDENT. Please. I just wanted ... I was looking at the shirt. Considering you ... I know you have no money. Or we pay you so little, rather. And you have such nice things. Can I see it? Please?

(He takes the lining between finger and thumb.)

AU PAIR. What's wrong with it?

STUDENT. Nothing. It's the most beautiful blue.

AU PAIR. Sir?

STUDENT. I mean it. I'm telling the truth. *(He puts his arm round her waist and draws her to him. She leans back as he unbuttons her blouse a little and kisses her chest.)* Your skin is beautiful. It's white.

AU PAIR. Now that's just flattery.

STUDENT. Nothing wrong with flattery, is there?

AU PAIR. No. Flattery is no harm

(She sighs under his kisses.)

STUDENT. What a beautiful sound ...

AU PAIR. Sir ...

(He has suddenly dropped to her feet, still nervous.)

STUDENT. And what beautiful shoes. Blue as well. What do you call them? Indigo?

AU PAIR. Cobalt.

STUDENT. Are they ... I mean, what I'm asking, did you get them from the same shop?

(He has wrapped himself round her knees.)

AU PAIR. Sir, if the doorbell rings ...

STUDENT. The bell won't ring.

AU PAIR. At least close the shutters.

(He goes across and pulls the blinds. The hot afternoon light slats through from outside, their faces in darkness. He looks at her from across the room.)

STUDENT. Why are you shy?

AU PAIR. You think I'm shy?

STUDENT. Anyone who looks like you has no reason to be embarrassed. If I looked like you, I wouldn't be shy. If I smelt like you. *(There is a pause. Neither of them move.)* The other evening, the bathroom door wasn't closed. You'd fallen asleep in the bath.

(They look at each other, not moving.)

AU PAIR. I'm ashamed.

STUDENT. I've seen you already. I'm half-way there, I'm already half-way there ...

(He moves quickly across and pushes her decisively onto the butcher's block. Then he climbs on top of her. He starts to pull her skirt up, clambering over her.)

AU PAIR. What if the bell rings, what if your friend comes ...

STUDENT. My friend won't come ...

AU PAIR. What if he does?

STUDENT. Let him ring. Don't go to the door. Just leave him. Don't go to the door.

AU PAIR. Down a bit. What if he comes? What if your friend

comes?

STUDENT. He won't come.

(Music engulfs them. Darkness. The projected slide reads: FORTY-FIVE SECONDS.)

• • • • •

(The music stops. The doorbell rings insistently.)

STUDENT. Shit! Oh, shit, shit, shit! *It rings again.)* Can you go? Go and look through the letterbox.

AU PAIR. What?

STUDENT. It may just be a beggar.

AU PAIR. You're joking.

STUDENT. I'm telling you: go and take a look.

(The AU PAIR pulls down her skirt and goes out. The STUDENT pulls up his trousers and opens the blinds. The light is liquid now, yellow. The AU PAIR returns.)

AU PAIR. Whoever it was, they've gone.

STUDENT. Are you sure?

AU PAIR. Of course I'm sure.

STUDENT. Do you think it was my friend.

(He seems restless. The AU PAIR doesn't notice and moves toward him again.)

AU PAIR. Well, we'll just never know.

(He looks down.)

STUDENT. I'm going to get a coffee.

AU PAIR. What?

STUDENT. I think I'd better go. I think I'd better be going. I'm going to the café. *(The AU PAIR just looks at him.)* I mean it. If my friend calls …

AU PAIR. He won't call …

STUDENT. If my friend does call ...
AU PAIR. He won't.

(There is a pause. The STUDENT is quite angry.)

STUDENT. If he does. I am saying, Marie, *if* he does ... if he does, please tell him where I am. Which will be in the café. *(He pauses a moment.)* I mean, if you could do your job.
AU PAIR. Sir.

(They stare at each other.)

4. THE STUDENT AND THE MARRIED WOMAN

(The STUDENT's bedroom. It's evening. A classic student tip, the walls maroon and festooned with posters of rock stars. The bed is covered in garish, disorderly sheets. There are books, records, discarded clothes, a dartboard. The student comes in, throwing down a load of books and a plastic bag, tearing off his clothes, grabbing a clean shirt and a pair of trousers. He stuffs his discarded clothes under the bed. From the plastic bag, he takes out a bottle of cognac and a foil-wrapped container, which he opens. Inside are a selection of frozen hors d'oeuvres: vol au vents, little meatballs, prawns on sticks. He fussily moves them around on the little tray to make them look more impressive, then sets them down beside the cognac. He takes a swig from the bottle.)

(As he does so, the doorbell rings outside. He goes to the bedroom door, opens it, listens. Someone has got to it before him. So he sits down in a chair with a book, trying to look casual. The MARRIED WOMAN comes in. In her early thirties, she has tried to disguise her arrival by wearing extremely tight trousers, a big shapeless coat, a scarf wrapped round her head and dark glasses. She looks like a cross between Jackie Onassis and the Invisible Man. She stands a moment with her left hand on her heart, as if mastering an overwhelming emotion.)

MARRIED WOMAN. My God!
STUDENT. I know. I'm sorry.
MARRIED WOMAN. That was terrifying.
STUDENT. I know.

(He gets up to move towards her, but she presses herself with her back to the door.)

MARRIED WOMAN. I never want to do that again.

STUDENT. No.

(She stands, recovering.)

MARRIED WOMAN. I thought ... if I came, your house would be empty. You promised.

STUDENT. Yes. I didn't think. The au pair. *(He takes a step towards her.)* It's all right, I know for a fact, she doesn't read the papers.

MARRIED WOMAN. I should hope not. I can stay five minutes.

(She moves quickly across the room. The STUDENT clears the chair of assorted student garbage and cleans it quickly with his hand. She sits. He frowns slightly.)

STUDENT. The problem is, I can't actually see you ...
MARRIED WOMAN. What
STUDENT. I mean with the glasses.
MARRIED WOMAN. Oh.

(She takes her glasses off.)

STUDENT. And the scarf.

(He takes off her scarf. She does not resist.)

MARRIED WOMAN. What's wrong?
STUDENT. It's the first time we've ever been alone.

(He inclines his head to kiss her but she moves a step away.)

MARRIED WOMAN. You asked me to visit you. I'm visiting. You simply don't understand ...
STUDENT. No ...
MARRIED WOMAN. The press in this country ...
STUDENT. Oh the press yes ...
MARRIED WOMAN. They have no values. They have no re-

spect.

(The STUDENT frowns, murmuring assent.)

STUDENT. Absolutely disgusting.

MARRIED WOMAN. It's so ridiculously hot in here!

STUDENT. That's because you've got your coat on.

MARRIED WOMAN. Then take it off. *(He comes round behind her and unbuttons her coat. He takes it to put it on the chair with her other things.)* Is this your room?

STUDENT. It is.

MARRIED WOMAN. Is this where you work? I shan't come again. And now I must go.

STUDENT. Emma!

MARRIED WOMAN. I mean it. I really do mean it. I'm friends with your parents, for God's sake.

STUDENT. So?

MARRIED WOMAN. We go skiing together.

(He looks at her a moment.)

STUDENT. Do you want a brandy?

MARRIED WOMAN. Yes. But get me some water first.

STUDENT. I'm sorry?

MARRIED WOMAN. A glass of water. You do have a kitchen, don't you?

STUDENT. Yes. *(He hasn't moved.)* Have a brandy instead.

(The MARRIED WOMAN watches as he pours cognac into a tooth-mug.)

MARRIED WOMAN. I thought I could do it and I can't.

STUDENT. Why? Isn't this what we want. We're together. We're in a room. For once without your husband's eyes boring into us ... *(At once he retracts.)* All right, sorry, I shouldn't have mentioned him ...

MARRIED WOMAN. You aren't married. You understand

nothing. *(The STUDENT gives her the brandy.)* I was coming up the stairs, I saw myself ...

STUDENT. Emma, I know how unhappy you are.

MARRIED WOMAN. Do you?

STUDENT. Yes, I do. I know your husband's world. Politics! My God! How could anyone be happy ... someone of your intelligence, your sensibility ... how could you be happy in a world of presentation and lies? *(The student is suddenly angry.)* What do you think this is? Some squalid assignation?

(She looks at him, directly.)

MARRIED WOMAN. What is it, then?

STUDENT. This is love. *(He nods slightly at his own admission.)* Jesus. I mean, this is it. It's love. I'm in fucking love. I can't live without you. It's true. Maybe I sound naive. Well I am. I am naive. *(The MARRIED WOMAN has taken a vol au vent from the foil container.)* Life's not a rehearsal. We're only here once.

MARRIED WOMAN. And how many women have you said that to?

STUDENT. Well, none. At least since I met you.

MARRIED WOMAN. Ah well, that's something ... *(They both smile.)* Anton, you promised ...

STUDENT. What did I promise? What did I promise exactly?

(There is a pause.)

MARRIED WOMAN. Take off my clothes.

(He fumbles a moment.)

STUDENT. Let me just ... how does this ...
MARRIED WOMAN. Let me do it, all right?

(He gets off the bed. She is wearing a body stocking under her clothes.)

STUDENT. What are you wearing?

MARRIED WOMAN. It's a body stocking. Madonna wears them. *(She gets into the bed in the body stocking.)* My God, it's cold in here.

STUDENT. It'll warm up quickly.

MARRIED WOMAN. Well that's rather up to you, isn't it? *(The STUDENT, undressing, is disturbed by this remark. The MARRIED WOMAN has undressed under the sheets.)* Come, come to bed, Anton.

STUDENT. I'm coming …

MARRIED WOMAN. There's a smell of honey …*(He gets into the bed, taking her in his arms.)* Oh Anton …

STUDENT. Emma …

(Music engulfs them. Darkness. The projected slide reads: 0 MINUTES.)
· · · · ·
(The MARRIED WOMAN is sitting at the side of the room. The STUDENT is in the bed.)

STUDENT. It's my fault. I'm sorry. It isn't you. I knew this would happen. Emma? *(She doesn't reply.)* I read an article.

MARRIED WOMAN. An article?

STUDENT. Some of the most famous men in history have had this particular experience.

MARRIED WOMAN. Ah.

STUDENT. Churchill. Regardless. Julius Caesar. (*The MARRIED WOMAN is frowning slightly.*) I'm not saying it makes me feel better. It doesn't. As you say, it doesn't matter, but even so.

MARRIED WOMAN. No. Though to be fair, you did promise me you wouldn't do anything and you've stuck to your promise …

STUDENT. Emma …

MARRIED WOMAN. This man is as good as his word!

STUDENT. That isn't funny.

MARRIED WOMAN. No one can say you didn't warn me.

STUDENT. What is this? Is this some sort of joke?

MARRIED WOMAN. No, for goodness' sake. It's just … do we have to be so bloody serious?

STUDENT. No, of course not.

MARRIED WOMAN. I didn't think it happened with young men, that's all. I thought it happened with clapped-out older men. Or men who haven't got any shagging left in them.

(The STUDENT frowns, trying to ignore this sudden vulgarity.)

STUDENT. Another thing, I tell you, I met this stockbroker. He'd had to wait fifteen years for the woman he loved — she was married, or something. And when they did finally get to be together, they just lay side by side. For six whole nights, they did nothing. They just cried.

MARRIED WOMAN. Both of them?

STUDENT. They cried for joy.

MARRIED WOMAN. Do you think that's true of all stockbrokers, or just this one, because ...

STUDENT. What is this?

MARRIED WOMAN. I think I may avoid stockbrokers in future. If all they can offer is communal weeping.

(He is suddenly raising his voice.)

STUDENT. Honestly, this whole thing seems to have cheered you up in some way...

MARRIED WOMAN. Not at all...

STUDENT. In some obscure way, you seem in very good spirits.

MARRIED WOMAN. I'm not.

STUDENT. I thought women were meant to reassure men on these occasions.

MARRIED WOMAN. Are they?

STUDENT. I thought they were meant to put it lightly aside and make them feel better.

MARRIED WOMAN. So?

STUDENT. I'm feeling worse.

(She relents a little, going across to reassure him.)

MARRIED WOMAN. Look, it's fine. We're friends. We're ...

what's that word? Comrades.

STUDENT. Oh for God's sake!

MARRIED WOMAN. You said it first. You said it! "Let's be comrades" you said ...

STUDENT. Did I?

MARRIED WOMAN. I couldn't believe it, I'd never met anyone who used that word seriously. *(She suddenly changes tack.)* And now I have to go ...

STUDENT. Emma, please ...

MARRIED WOMAN. I have to!

STUDENT. Just stay five minutes. Please!

MARRIED WOMAN. All right, but only ... only if ... you make me a promise.

STUDENT. What promise?

MARRIED WOMAN. Trust me.

(There's a pause.)

STUDENT. What do I do.

MARRIED WOMAN. Trust me. I know more than you. Lie completely still. *(He lies back. She stands at the end of the bed.)* That's it. If you move, then I leave. Just lie. Lie.

(She stands above him, about to solve the problem. Music engulfs them. Darkness. The projected slide reads: THIRTY-TWO MINUTES.)

• • • • •

(Darkness. Silence.)

MARRIED WOMAN. Oh my beautiful boy. *(The MARRIED WOMAN turns on the light.)* What time is it?

STUDENT. *(looking at his watch.)* Eight.

MARRIED WOMAN. Eight, my God!

(She wraps the sheet round herself and starts urgently to gather up her things.)

MARRIED WOMAN. I know it. I just know it.

STUDENT. Know what?

MARRIED WOMAN. Tonight. Tonight will be the night when for once he comes home early. Where are my shoes?

(The STUDENT has got out of bed and holds out her shoes.)

STUDENT. Here.

MARRIED WOMAN. You don't get it, do you? You don't understand. This could be the end for both of us.

STUDENT. Why?

MARRIED WOMAN. Because I'm a hopeless liar, that's why. I'm hopeless.

STUDENT. Then you'll have to get better.

MARRIED WOMAN. And all this for you, for a man like you. Here, give me a kiss. *(They embrace, she holding her clothes, then she runs into the bathroom, very happy.)* A hopeless liar, and hopelessly shy. *(She closes the door. He starts to pull on some trousers, then stops and goes to eat several hors d'oeuvres. She speaks from inside the bathroom.)* Anton!

STUDENT. Yes?

MARRIED WOMAN. *(off.)* Thank God we didn't just cry. *(He smiles contentedly.)* How will it be? When I see you across a room one day?

STUDENT. What do you mean, one day? We're meant to be at the rally tomorrow.

MARRIED WOMAN. *(off.)* What rally?

STUDENT. We're all going. Your husband's speaking at the rally.

MARRIED WOMAN. *(off.)* I won't go. Are you mad? *(She reappears. She grabs at some hors d'oeuvres as she finishes dressing.)* I couldn't possibly. I'd never survive.

STUDENT. I'll see you tomorrow.

MARRIED WOMAN. It's out of the question.

STUDENT. Then the day after. Get here by six.

MARRIED WOMAN. Can I get a cab on the street?

STUDENT. Sure. It's a deal. The day after tomorrow. Be here at six.

MARRIED WOMAN. There's no deal. We'll discuss it tomorrow. At the rally.

(He embraces her.)

> STUDENT. My angel!
> MARRIED WOMAN. Be careful of my hair.
> STUDENT. Tomorrow, politics, then next day, love.
> MARRIED WOMAN. Goodbye.
> STUDENT. *(suddenly worried.)* What … I mean, I'm just ask-
> ing: what *will* you tell him?
> MARRIED WOMAN. Don't ask. Don't even ask.

(The STUDENT kisses her for a last time. She goes. He is left alone. He sits down on the sofa and eats some more hors d'oeuvres.)

> STUDENT. I'm fucking a married woman.

5. THE MARRIED WOMAN AND THE POLITICIAN

(A wealthy bedroom. The MARRIED WOMAN is lying in bed, working on papers. There are two single beds. Above them, some modern paintings. The POLITICIAN, early forties, comes into the room, his tie is loose round his neck, and his sleeves are rolled up. He looks tired. The MARRIED WOMAN does not look up.)

MARRIED WOMAN. Have you stopped already?

POLITICIAN. I'm exhausted.

MARRIED WOMAN. You never stop before one.

POLITICIAN. The government of the country ... *(He smiles, self-satirizing.)* Besides, I felt lonely.

MARRIED WOMAN. Oh really.

(He puts his hand in front of her eyes.)

POLITICIAN. Don't read any more. You'll hurt your eyes. *(She doesn't move.)* For some time now, I've wanted to talk to you, Emma. To thank you, really.

MARRIED WOMAN. Thank me?

POLITICIAN. Yes. I know there are times when I'm close to you, and times when I'm not. Sometimes, I just have to take one step back. I have to withdraw ...

MARRIED WOMAN. Yes...

POLITICIAN. It's because of the work ...

MARRIED WOMAN. I'm sure.

POLITICIAN. The irregular hours, the separations. *(He gestures toward his single bed.)* But, on the other hand, there is compensation.

MARRIED WOMAN. What's that?

POLITICIAN. These moments when we find each other again. *(He sits on her bed.)* I remember someone saying to me years ago: a real marriage is always moving. It's never still. At any one moment you're either moving closer together or moving further apart.

MARRIED WOMAN. Which at the moment?

POLITICIAN. Oh, closer. *(There's a moment's pause.)* I was remembering how we started ...

MARRIED WOMAN. Ah yes ...

POLITICIAN. How things were at the beginning. If we'd gone on like that, we would have both gone mad.

MARRIED WOMAN. Would we?

POLITICIAN. Of course. If we'd gone on as we started in Venice ...

MARRIED WOMAN. Venice!

POLITICIAN. Yes. My God! *(He moves a little closer to her.)* If we'd gone on like that for ...

MARRIED WOMAN. Months, you mean?

POLITICIAN. Yes.

MARRIED WOMAN. Instead of weeks?

POLITICIAN. Exactly. I think we'd have gone up in flames.

MARRIED WOMAN. Perhaps.

(He shakes his head at the narrow escape.)

POLITICIAN. I don't know. I've watched so many marriages conceived in bed, lived out in bed, and, let's face it, finished off in bed, everything over in a space of a few years ...

MARRIED WOMAN. Yes ...

POLITICIAN. Bed the only criterion, bed the only place of contact, bed the only thing holding things together ...

MARRIED WOMAN. Yes ...

POLITICIAN. Thank God ours isn't like that.

(There is a moment's pause.)

MARRIED WOMAN. No.

POLITICIAN. You have to be friends, don't you? Friends as well as lovers. You know what I think's important? What's most important of all?

MARRIED WOMAN. No.

POLITICIAN. A sense of humor.

MARRIED WOMAN. Ah.

POLITICIAN. If you can laugh together. As we laugh together ...

MARRIED WOMAN. Sure.

POLITICIAN. Then there's a basis. Then there's something solid. A woman you can laugh with.

MARRIED WOMAN. Is that what I am?

POLITICIAN. Among other things, yes.

(He looks at her fondly.)

MARRIED WOMAN. Are you coming to bed?

POLITICIAN. I am. *(He kisses her on the forehead and then gets up. He takes three identical little mobile phones from his pockets and sets them down in a row on the sideboard, like hairbrushes. Then starts to change.)* It's quite frightening, you know, in my work. I look back. Personal liberation was such a wonderful idea, but here we are, thirty years later, and governments have to deal with the consequences... *(He takes off his shoes and socks.)* Social disintegration, homelessness, cities falling apart, social services over-stretched. I heard of a young woman the other day, five children by five different fathers. And behaving as if somehow that's her God-given right. And the rest of us have to care for those children. *(He stands in his boxer shorts.)* Oh, yes, freedom's a wonderful thing, but I sometimes think you should have to pass a test to prove you deserve it.

MARRIED WOMAN. And do you deserve it?

POLITICIAN. Well I think I probably do, yes.

MARRIED WOMAN. Goodness. *(They both smile.)* The funny thing is, you tell me so little about your own past ...

POLITICIAN. Me?

MARRIED WOMAN. Yes.

POLITICIAN. Do I?

MARRIED WOMAN. About your own freedom, I mean.

POLITICIAN. I must change.

(He goes to the bathroom.)

MARRIED WOMAN. It's so strange. We've been together eight

years and in those years have you ever talked to me about what your life was like before?

POLITICIAN. *(off.)* Of course I have.

MARRIED WOMAN. But I mean, really talked?

(The POLITICIAN returns, in pajamas.)

POLITICIAN. You know all the names…

MARRIED WOMAN. Of course …

POLITICIAN. The list. Haven't we been through the list? Who I was close to.

MARRIED WOMAN. But the *kind* of life. I know very little.

POLITICIAN. It's not a life I want to think about. *(He gets into bed.)* I'm so much happier now.

MARRIED WOMAN. Are you?

POLITICIAN. Of course. *(He shakes his head, appalled at his memories.)* My God, all that confusion, all that uncertainty …

MARRIED WOMAN. Were there so many then?

POLITICIAN. You've asked me this before. Why does it matter?

MARRIED WOMAN. It matters. I want to know. Tell me.

POLITICIAN. Does it? Does the past matter? *(He pauses a moment, reluctant to go on.)* Emma, you've lived a sheltered life … *(He smiles as if to anticipate.)* Compared with me at least, let's say compared with me, so the point is, most of us know, there's a certain kind of woman …

MARRIED WOMAN. Is there?

POLITICIAN. Of course. You know what I'm saying. In their hearts everyone knows there are two kinds of women …

MARRIED WOMAN. Two?

POLITICIAN. Only you're not meant to say so. And I am someone who spent many years of my life — too many perhaps — with that first kind of woman.

MARRIED WOMAN. And what kind of woman is that?

POLITICIAN. Oh come on, do I really need to spell it out? *(The MARRIED WOMAN just looks at him, not answering. He's provoked.)* The kind of woman you just sleep with. *(The MARRIED WOMAN makes no reaction.)* Well, look …

MARRIED WOMAN. I see ...

POLITICIAN. It's fine when you're young ...

MARRIED WOMAN. Of course.

POLITICIAN. When you're young, it's natural. It's part of growing up. But it's not ... look, it's not a life. It's not a life like we have. With children.

MARRIED WOMAN. I want more children.

POLITICIAN. Well, good.

(He waits a minute.)

MARRIED WOMAN. What's happened to the women?

POLITICIAN. Why?

MARRIED WOMAN. Are you still in touch?

POLITICIAN. Of course not. Don't be ridiculous. Do you think now that I'm married ... do you think I wouldn't have told you?

MARRIED WOMAN. Well ...

POLITICIAN. I tell you everything.

(He looks her straight in the eye.)

MARRIED WOMAN. Did you sleep with married women?

POLITICIAN. What?

MARRIED WOMAN. Did you sleep with married women?

POLITICIAN. Emma, I never broke up a marriage.

MARRIED WOMAN. Ah ...

POLITICIAN. Now that is something quite other. I'm sorry but that is something quite different.

(She looks at him a moment.)

MARRIED WOMAN. You think so?

POLITICIAN. Of course. It's a basic principle. Everyone has the right to follow their own ... wotdyumcallems, their own needs, their own desires, but they have no right to destroy other peoples' happiness. Isn't that right?

MARRIED WOMAN. I don't know.

(The POLITICIAN is frowning.)

POLITICIAN. You don't sound sure.
MARRIED WOMAN. No.
POLITICIAN. Is that because you have friends who do it? Do some of your friends sleep with married men?
MARRIED WOMAN. I think so.
POLITICIAN. And what do they feel?
MARRIED WOMAN. I don't know.
POLITICIAN. How do they defend it?

(She shrugs slightly.)

MARRIED WOMAN. I don't think they have to *defend* it.
POLITICIAN. How do they live with all the lying, the deceit? The sheer level of organization. Being where you shouldn't be, at times that don't fit! The danger, the strain. And for what? Just that one extra moment of happiness. That one short moment of bliss.
MARRIED WOMAN. Hmm. *(There's a pause.)* Are you sure you never did it yourself? Tell me.

(The POLITICIAN hesitates.)

POLITICIAN. Look, if I tell you, you won't take it badly?
MARRIED WOMAN. Go on.
POLITICIAN. A woman I knew when I was young.

(There's a silence.)

MARRIED WOMAN. She was married.
POLITICIAN. Yes.
MARRIED WOMAN. How long did you know her?
POLITICIAN. Long enough.
MARRIED WOMAN. I see.
POLITICIAN. Some months.
MARRIED WOMAN. Did you love her very much?
POLITICIAN. Yes. If a man can love a liar.

(There is another silence.)

    MARRIED WOMAN. And where is she now?
    POLITICIAN. Oh ...
    MARRIED WOMAN. No, tell me.
    POLITICIAN. Do you want me to tell you?
    MARRIED WOMAN. Yes.
    POLITICIAN. She died. *(He is thoughtful now.)* Not happily. Unhappily. In unhappy circumstances. She died in a god-awful mess of drink and obsession. Which is, to be honest, what I knew would happen. There was something tragic in her. Something not right. And that is what appealed. That is why ... I fell so hard.

(She is watching him.)

    MARRIED WOMAN. What was her name?
    POLITICIAN. Estelle.
    MARRIED WOMAN. Estelle.

(They both think a minute.)

    POLITICIAN. But I have only known real love once. And that is with you. *(He reaches and takes her in his arms.)* Let me kiss you.

(They kiss.)

    MARRIED WOMAN. Charlie ...
    POLITICIAN. I feel so safe in your arms, so happy.
    MARRIED WOMAN. Do you?
    POLITICIAN. If only we'd met when I was younger. I would never have needed to know anyone else. You're a beautiful woman, you hear me? Beautiful ...

(He turns the light out. Music engulfs them. Darkness. The projected slide reads: FIFTEEN MINUTES.)

• • • • •

(The music stops. They are lying in each others' arms.)

MARRIED WOMAN. You know what I'm thinking of?

POLITICIAN. No.

MARRIED WOMAN. Of Venice.

POLITICIAN. Ah yes.

MARRIED WOMAN. Of our first night together.

POLITICIAN. Yes. *(There is a pause.)* What is it? Tell me.

MARRIED WOMAN. If all our nights could be like that. If you could always love me like that.

POLITICIAN. Yes. *(There is a pause.)* What's wonderful about marriage: that there will be time for everything. I mean, not everyone has Venice, even as a memory.

MARRIED WOMAN. No.

(They lie, both awake.)

POLITICIAN. Goodnight, my darling.

MARRIED WOMAN. Goodnight.

6. THE POLITICIAN AND THE MODEL

(A room in the Metropole. It is a desperately fashionable minimalist hotel, pared away to essential surfaces of marble and glass: a high-class knocking shop. The POLITICIAN is sitting back with a cigar contentedly on the sofa, having finished a lavish dinner. With him is the MODEL. She looks about seventeen, in a micro-skirt and skinny jumper. She is spooning at a chocolate ice cream in a pretentiously large glass and dancing happily to the rock video on the television. The POLITICIAN watches her.)

POLITICIAN. How is it?

MODEL. It's great.

POLITICIAN. Can I get you another? You've no champagne left. Here. *(He pours her another glass. She drinks it straight down.)* And now I'd like a kiss.

(She kisses him on the sofa, then turns back to her dancing.)

MODEL. You must think I'm a slut.

POLITICIAN. Why?

MODEL. Coming straight to the hotel.

POLITICIAN. I don't think you're a slut.

(He tries to pull her toward him.)

MODEL. Hey!

POLITICIAN. That wasn't the first time I'd seen you.

MODEL. I guessed that.

POLITICIAN. We could have gone for a walk first. If that would have made things more respectable.

MODEL. Had you been following me?

POLITICIAN. I'm not telling you anything.

MODEL. Plenty of men do.
POLITICIAN. I'm sure.
MODEL. I never speak to any of them.
POLITICIAN. No? You spoke to me.
MODEL. And are you complaining?

(He kisses her violently.)

POLITICIAN. You taste of pudding.
MODEL. I just have sweet lips.
POLITICIAN. Really? Have men told you that before?
MODEL. Some.
POLITICIAN. How many?
MODEL. I'm not saying.
POLITICIAN. I want to know. It's important. I want to know.
MODEL. Guess.
POLITICIAN. Fifty?

(She breaks away.)

MODEL. Fifty? Why don't you just make it five hundred? Fifty!
POLITICIAN. I'm sorry. It was a guess.
MODEL. Guess again.
POLITICIAN. Five.
MODEL. I am seventeen, you know. I'm not a total innocent.

(She dances on. The POLITICIAN frowns slightly.)

POLITICIAN. You are desperately thin, my dear.
MODEL. If you're a model, you have to look awful. That's the job.
POLITICIAN. I can't believe you've got that quite right.
MODEL. You have to look sort of awful but sort of beautiful as well.
POLITICIAN. It's a balance, you mean?
MODEL. Beautiful underneath.
POLITICIAN. What does your boyfriend think? You must have

a boyfriend. An attractive girl like you.

MODEL. Why are you asking? Why do you want to know?

(The POLITICIAN hesitates, phrasing it carefully.)

POLITICIAN. It's simple. I find myself ... powerfully attracted to you.

(She looks at him a moment, then gets some coke out of her handbag.)

MODEL. Do you want some?

POLITICIAN. No thank you. *(She empties it onto a little mirror. The POLITICIAN looks a little nervous.)* Who was he then?

MODEL. Who?

POLITICIAN. Your last boyfriend.

MODEL. Are you still on that? *(She looks up at him for a moment from preparing her coke.)* He looked like you. As it happens.

POLITICIAN. Really?

MODEL. Yes. Very like you, in fact.

(She goes back to her preparations.)

POLITICIAN. If you say so.

MODEL. You talk like him, too. "If you say so." And you have the same way of looking.

POLITICIAN. What way is that?

MODEL. The way you're looking now. *(She looks up at him again.)* Don't. Don't look at me like that. *(He moves across and takes her in his arms, kissing her passionately. It's suddenly electric. Then she breaks free.)* I'm going to go after this.

POLITICIAN. Why?

MODEL. Because I've got to get home, obviously. What will my mum say?

POLITICIAN. You still live with your mother?

MODEL. There's five of us. That's why I've got to get back. I've got sisters still at school.

POLITICIAN. And how old are they?

MODEL. There's one who's thirteen. I caught her out on a date the other day. I couldn't believe it. The little slut!

POLITICIAN. What did you do?

MODEL. I beat the shit out of her when she got home. *(She sniffs a line of coke.)* That's what I'm saying. If I don't give them some discipline, who does?

(She snorts a second line.)

POLITICIAN. The strange thing is, you remind me of someone, too.

MODEL. Do I? *(She sits back, luxuriating, closing her eyes.)* Who do I remind you of?

POLITICIAN. Someone I knew when I was young.

(She is quiet. Her eyes are still closed.)

MODEL. You haven't told me your name.

POLITICIAN. Charles.

MODEL. *(laughs.)* Are you really called Charles?

POLITICIAN. Why? Was that his name as well? *(There is a silence.)* You still haven't told me who he was.

MODEL. He was a cunt. He was a cunt, or why else would he have left me.

POLITICIAN. You were in love? *(She is silent.)* I thought your eyes were green, but they're blue really.

MODEL. And isn't blue good enough for you? *(He takes this as a cue. He moves to kiss her. But before he can she holds out her hand which is full of pills.)* Here. Take one of these.

POLITICIAN. Which one?

MODEL. A white one. *(He pops one in his mouth.)* Two.

(He takes both. Then, to amuse her, takes another at random.)

POLITICIAN. Anything you say. *(They kiss.)* When did you meet this man?

MODEL. I can't remember. I can't remember anything. The

room's going round.

POLITICIAN. Hold on to me. Hold on tight. *(Her eyes are closed. He slips to the floor, putting his head between her legs.)* How is that? Is that good?

MODEL. I don't know what you're doing. *(She leans back.)* God knows where it came from. It was the usual guy. He'd got it from some other guy and he said. And he said. And he said. He said he'd got it from another guy...

(She puts her head back as music engulfs them. Darkness. The projected slide reads: TWO HOURS TWENTY-EIGHT MINUTES.)

• • • • •

(Light creeps back. The POLITICIAN is cringing against the wall in his trousers and shirt, very alert. The MODEL is lying on her back, abandoned like a dishcloth.)

MODEL. Why are you so far away? Why don't you come here? *(He turns and looks at her. He is plainly disturbed.)* Jesus, where did I get that stuff?

POLITICIAN. Good question.

MODEL. I would never have done it ...

POLITICIAN. Ah that's very flattering, I must say. It was the drugs, was it?

(Suddenly the MODEL protests with a real, shocking vehemence.)

MODEL. I don't do this! I don't fucking do this! I don't sleep with men I don't know.

POLITICIAN. Of course you don't. I know you don't. I can see that.

MODEL. It's not me. It's not what I do.

POLITICIAN. Well that's good. I mean, that's good from all points of view. *(He shifts, uncomfortable.)* That's what I was asking earlier, why I want to know. Who else ...

MODEL. Oh God, are you still going on about that?

POLITICIAN. I'm just asking.

MODEL. What for? *(There's a pause.)* What have I done? Have I done something wrong?

POLITICIAN. No. On the contrary. In fact … I was hoping I might see you again.

MODEL. Oh yes?

POLITICIAN. Maybe not here. Maybe some sort of place I might find for you.

(She looks at him a moment.)

MODEL. You're married, aren't you?

POLITICIAN. What makes you say that?

MODEL. That's just how it looks.

POLITICIAN. Would it bother you if I were?

MODEL. What do you do?

POLITICIAN. I'm a politician. I help run the country.

MODEL. Uh-huh.

(Her gaze doesn't waver.)

POLITICIAN. Would it worry you? If it turned out you'd been with a married man?

MODEL. Why should it worry me?

POLITICIAN. That you'd helped him cheat on his wife.

MODEL. Well, I'm sure she cheats on you.

(The POLITICIAN laughs.)

POLITICIAN. Hardly.

MODEL. What makes you so sure?

POLITICIAN. I really don't think it's very likely.

MODEL. Don't you? If she's anything like the women I know, then …

POLITICIAN. You know nothing, You know *fuck nothing! You know absolutely nothing at all!*

(He has suddenly shouted at her. He gets up, very disturbed.)

MODEL. I thought you said you weren't married.

POLITICIAN. Whether I'm married or not, you plainly know nothing about ... about another kind of world to your own.

(There's a silence while he recovers.)

MODEL. I didn't know you were married. I was just talking, all right? I was just talking.

POLITICIAN. My fault. I'm unused to the pills. *(He goes over and sits beside her on the sofa.)* Listen, I need to see you again.

MODEL. Do you?

POLITICIAN. Of course. But for me, it's not easy. If we come to an arrangement, I have to say, in the nature of things I can't be watching you.

MODEL. I don't suppose you can.

POLITICIAN. I can't be checking up all the time *(He looks at her a moment.)* I'm not talking about the moral side of things. That doesn't bother me. And, for myself, I shall have to be careful, meaning discreet. The press in this country is a scandal. It's completely out of control. But beyond that what I'm talking about is something else. *(There's a pause.)* The world as it now is. As it has become. I'll be frank. I'm talking about hygiene. *(She looks at him in silence.)* That's not unreasonable.

MODEL. Ah.

POLITICIAN. I can get us a place. It could even be a place where you lived. If you wanted to live by yourself. *(He smiles.)* Next time we'll be somewhere else.

MODEL. Maybe.

POLITICIAN. Where we can't be disturbed.

MODEL. Maybe.

(He looks at her from across the room.)

POLITICIAN. Kelly, I'm offering you a life of your own. Independence. *(She doesn't reply.)* Isn't that what women want?

7. THE MODEL AND THE PLAYWRIGHT

(A studio in a bohemian part of town, self-consciously artistic, full of books and CDs. A large, modern writing desk is covered with papers and scripts. There is a piano at the back of the room. The curtains are drawn and the room is in half-dark. The PLAY-WRIGHT opens the door, letting the MODEL in behind him. He is in his early thirties, rather intense. She is tottering on high heels, and a little bit the worse for wear.)

PLAYWRIGHT. How is it?
MODEL. It's beautiful. But I can't see a thing.
PLAYWRIGHT. Your eyes'll get used to it. Your beautiful eyes.

(He kisses them in the darkness.)

MODEL. Hmm. My beautiful eyes won't have time to get used to it. I'm off in a mo.

(He ignores the remark.)

PLAYWRIGHT. Let's have candles, shall we? There was a power-cut a few years ago, and afterwards I thought: why go back to electricity? Everything is cast in a magical light. *(He has lit a candelabra, and now looks round, pleased with the effect.) He gestures towards the sofa.)* Sit down over there. Sleep if you want to.
MODEL. I'm not tired. Are you going to play the song?
PLAYWRIGHT. Well I am. It's a song of my own.
MODEL. Of your own? I thought you were a journalist.
PLAYWRIGHT. My God! What made you think that?

(She has taken her coat off and slumped onto the sofa. He has sat down at the piano stool, displeased.)

MODEL. You said …

PLAYWRIGHT. Jesus!

MODEL. At the party you said you were a writer. Aren't journalists writers?

PLAYWRIGHT. Hardly. I mean, generically, perhaps. Like rats are animals.

(She nods at his desk with its swish computer.)

MODEL. Is that what your computer's for?

PLAYWRIGHT. Oh yes, but I never use it. To me the feel of the pen on the paper is all-important.

MODEL. Huh. *(She waits a moment.)* You said you were going to play me this song you'd written.

PLAYWRIGHT. Did I say I'd written it?

MODEL. Yeah, you did actually.

PLAYWRIGHT. Did I write it? No. I helped write it, that's more accurate. Does it matter? No. Ultimately, is authorship important? Come on, the work exists. It's the work we should value, not the writer.

(He smiles contentedly.)

MODEL. Aren't you going to play the song?

PLAYWRIGHT. I am. It's called *THE BLUE ROOM.*

(He sits down at the piano.)

PLAYWRIGHT.

Blue, like blue like blue is how I'm feeling
Blew like how the wind blew all night long
And blew aside your cotton dress revealing
This, the opening of the opening of a song

You, like how you seemed at our first meeting
But are people ever truly what them seem?
For soon I felt that subtle, slight retreating

That marks the ending of the ending of a dream

I'm in the blue room
I'm in the blue
The dream was just a dream
It wasn't you

Hitch a passage to the moon on some Apollo
Get out a take a look at what you find
The earth looks kind of circular and hollow
And blue's the shade you'll see you've left behind

I'm in the blue room
I'm in the blue
The dream was just a dream
It wasn't you

Tell me why this lonely feeling hits me
That the person who I wanted wasn't you
And let me say, if politesse permits me.
I'm left with nothing save the color blue

(At the end the MODEL applauds, delighted.)

    MODEL. It's great.
    PLAYWRIGHT. Thank you.
    MODEL. I mean, it really is great. *(She frowns slightly.)* What sort of writer are you?
    PLAYWRIGHT. Do you really not know who I am?
    MODEL. No.
    PLAYWRIGHT. This is wonderful.
    MODEL. Why?
    PLAYWRIGHT. I mean, I love the idea. Are you serious?
    MODEL. Of course.
    PLAYWRIGHT. Do you mean … you really don't recognize me, do you?
    MODEL. No.

PLAYWRIGHT. Very good. *(He thinks about it a moment, pleased.)* What sort of writer am I? Yes, well, this is a very good question. This is something people have argued about. The work's not easy to put in a box.
MODEL. Ah.
PLAYWRIGHT. The work's won prizes.
MODEL. The work has?
PLAYWRIGHT. Well, I mean, I have.

(She frowns again.)

MODEL. Do you have any drugs?
PLAYWRIGHT. Drugs? I've run out. I write about them, of course. They're one of my defining subjects. But at the moment, no.
MODEL. My bra hurts.
PLAYWRIGHT. Take off your bra. Take anything off. It won't bother me.
MODEL. Thanks.

(She slips her bra off from under her jumper as he goes on talking.)

PLAYWRIGHT. Inevitably, I get labeled, as if I'm part of a movement. They call me a post-romantic. I know. It's just a shallow name the press dreamt up *(He thinks a moment.)* Restlessness. Longing. These things don't go away just because of what we call progress. We still search. We still pursue the ideal. We land. We cast off. With luck, we make waves. But finally we have no control of the tide. *(He is lost in thought. He turns.)* What did I say?
MODEL. What?
PLAYWRIGHT. What did I just say?
MODEL. Something about restlessness. Longing.
PLAYWRIGHT. That's right. What else?
MODEL. "No control of the tide."

(He has reached for a scrap of paper on the table and is making a note.)

PLAYWRIGHT. "... of the tide." Good. *(He puts his notebook aside.)* Do you want something to drink?

MODEL. I'd prefer something to eat. I'm starving. People think modelling's just swanning up and down.

PLAYWRIGHT. That's interesting. Where do you live?

MODEL. I've got a flat. Near the Centre.

PLAYWRIGHT. The centre? Really?

MODEL. Someone ... someone found it for me.

(He is very close. The candelabra on the piano throws their faces into shadow.)

PLAYWRIGHT. You're blushing. It's dark. But I can tell you're blushing. *(He puts his hand up to her cheek. She does not resist.)* Tell me more about yourself. Everything about you interests me. Have you ever been in love. *(He stops her before she answers.)* Don't tell me. Let me guess. *(She says nothing.)* And you miss him, don't you? *(She is beginning to cry.)* Oh I love it, I love it. Say something else. I'll take you away, I promise. Have you been to India?

MODEL. No.

PLAYWRIGHT. Let's go. We'll go to the Rajasthan. There are forts, can you imagine? Built over the cities. I'll put you on the battlements, and we'll fuck each other's brains out.

(He goes to collect the candelabra.)

MODEL. I wish I understood you. I wish I knew what you were saying.

PLAYWRIGHT. That I want to be with you. That I can't get enough of you. That everything about you ... your beautiful little jumper ... *(He puts the candelabra on the floor beside the sofa and starts kissing her breasts through the material.)* Your naïve untutored little skirt ... and the thought of the paper-thin, onion-skin, fragile yellow papyrus of your knickers ...

MODEL. What?

PLAYWRIGHT. I'm known for my enormous vocabulary. My capacious vocabulary! The egregious, rapacious, dithyrambic immensity of my individual lexicon … *(He suddenly raises his voice.)* Big words. My work is throbbing with big words! Trouser-bulging with polysllables! *(He reaches down and starts blowing out the candles.)* We'll go. We'll go together to Jaipur.

MODEL. Where?

PLAYWRIGHT. I worship you. I fucking worship you, my child.

(He reaches down and blows out the last candle. Music engulfs them. Darkness. The projected slide reads: FORTY-NINE MINUTES.)

• • • • •

(The music fades. Voices from the darkness.)

PLAYWRIGHT. That was wonderful

MODEL. Oh Robert …

PLAYWRIGHT. And only now shall I tell you my name. *(There is a pause.)* I'm Robert Phethean.

MODEL. Phethean?

PLAYWRIGHT. Yes. I knew you'd guessed. I could tell.

MODEL. I hadn't guessed. Really. I've never heard of you.

PLAYWRIGHT. Are you serious? Do you never go to the theatre?

MODEL. My aunt took me to *The Phantom of the Opera.*

PLAYWRIGHT. I said the *theatre.*

MODEL. I've never been asked.

PLAYWRIGHT. Well I shall ask you.

MODEL. Great. But I only like funny things.

PLAYWRIGHT. Do you mean comedy?

MODEL. Or scary things.

PLAYWRIGHT. Why's that? Have you never been to a proper play? A serious play?

MODEL. What's the point?

PLAYWRIGHT. Not even if it were by me? *(He gets up in the darkness from the sofa.)* I want to see you. I haven't seen you since we made love.

(He strikes a match to light a candle. She lies, unembarrassed.)

MODEL. Give me the cover.

PLAYWRIGHT. In a moment. *(He pulls back the cover from her naked body and stands over her, candle in hand.)* You are so beautiful. You're what I've been looking for. Total natural naked innocence.

MODEL. Ow! The wax is dripping. That bloody well hurts.

PLAYWRIGHT. I'm sorry. *(She covers herself up again. He laughs, still naked.)* You really didn't know I was Robert Phethean?

MODEL. I told you, I've never heard of you.

PLAYWRIGHT. Ah fame, fame! *(He shakes his head in ironic sadness.)* Fine, forget I'm a writer. Honestly. I'll be a shop assistant. I'll be a venture capitalist, if you like.

MODEL. I'm totally fucked. What are you talking about?

PLAYWRIGHT. Our future.

MODEL. What future?

PLAYWRIGHT. Let's just go, don't you think so? Do you have a few weeks?

MODEL. Of course not.

PLAYWRIGHT. Go and live in the woods. In the depth of the forest. It's what I've always wanted. Get away from all this. And then one day ... just look each other in the eye and say goodbye.

MODEL. Goodbye? Why? Why say goodbye?

PLAYWRIGHT. Because you're too much for me.

(He takes her once more in his arms, wrapped in the cover.)

MODEL. I'm cold. Hold me.

(He kisses her and looks at her kindly.)

PLAYWRIGHT. It's time you got dressed. *(He gathers up her clothes and he starts to dress her.)* Tell me, would you call yourself happy?

MODEL. Now?

PLAYWRIGHT. In general.

MODEL. I'm not unhappy.

PLAYWRIGHT. I'm not asking about your circumstances or even the men in your life. What I'm asking is: do you feel alive? Do you feel you're really living?

    MODEL. You don't have a comb, do you?

    PLAYWRIGHT. I do. *(He picks one up from the table and moves across to give it to her.)* You look astonishing.

    MODEL. Thank you.

(They are both still a moment, then she combs her hair.)

    PLAYWRIGHT. It's not nine yet. Why don't we eat?

    MODEL. It'll have be be quick.

    PLAYWRIGHT. I'll get you a ticket for my play.

    MODEL. Do.

    PLAYWRIGHT. It's sold out, of course. But I can get you one.

(She finishes combing, then turns towards him in the candlelight.)

    MODEL. I'm ready.

    PLAYWRIGHT. I'm looking at you and I'm thinking: if it could be like this. If it could always be like this.

(She looks down. Overwhelmed. He holds out an arm towards the door.)

    PLAYWRIGHT. After you.

8. THE PLAYWRIGHT AND THE ACTRESS

(A room in a country hotel, in rustic style. There is a large, old-fashioned bed at the center of the room and the dark walls are dimly seen to be hung with pictures. The room is dominated by a large window which is open. A huge net curtain billows and blows. At once the PLAYWRIGHT comes in carrying the AC-TRESS's luggage. She is magnificent, in her early forties, and splendidly assured. He puts the bag down and clicks vainly at the light switch.)

PLAYWRIGHT. Oh I don't believe it. The light doesn't work. Never mind. Look! There's a moon ... *(The ACTRESS has gone to the open window and dropped to her knees in front of the moon. The PLAYWRIGHT closes the door.)* What's wrong? *(The ACTRESS doesn't reply. The PLAYWRIGHT goes over and joins her.)* What on earth are you doing?

ACTRESS. What do you think I'm doing. I'm praying.

PLAYWRIGHT. I had no idea.

ACTRESS. I'm not a bloody heathen like you.

PLAYWRIGHT. Goodness.

ACTRESS. Come and kneel beside me, infidel. It'll do you good. *(He kneels and puts his arm round her.)* Oh sex, sex, sex ... *(She gets up.)* And who do you think I was praying to?

PLAYWRIGHT. Well, to God, I imagine.

ACTRESS. That's just where you're wrong. I was praying to you.

PLAYWRIGHT. Then why were you looking out of the window?

ACTRESS. What on earth are we doing? Where have you dragged me off to, you blatant seducer.

PLAYWRIGHT. It was your idea. The country! you kept saying.

ACTRESS. Well, wasn't I right.

PLAYWRIGHT. Of course. It's beautiful. Only an hour out of town and it's as if we're in paradise.

ACTRESS. It's bliss. You could write wonderful things here if you had any talent.

(He frowns, swallowing this insult as she goes and sits on the edge of the bed.)

PLAYWRIGHT. Have you been here before?
ACTRESS. Been here? I lived here.
PLAYWRIGHT. Really? Who with?
ACTRESS. With Fritz. With the magical Fritz. I adored him.
PLAYWRIGHT. Yes, so you said.
ACTRESS. Oh I'm sorry. Please, if I'm boring you, I'll go somewhere else.
PLAYWRIGHT. How could you bore me? I've never been less bored by anyone in my life. As long as you don't talk about Fritz. Let's make a rule. No Fritz.
ACTRESS. Well. Fritz was an episode.
PLAYWRIGHT. I'm glad you can see that.

(She looks at him a moment.)

ACTRESS. Come over and kiss me.

(They kiss.)

PLAYWRIGHT. You're going to laugh when I say this but I find in you a kind of total natural naked innocence. I mean it.
ACTRESS. You do talk more shit per square meter than any man I've ever met. And now goodnight.
PLAYWRIGHT. What do you mean?
ACTRESS. I'm off to bed. Can I have my bag, please?
PLAYWRIGHT. Here. Here it is. *(She takes out a small Madonna and puts it on the bedside table.)* And who's that?
ACTRESS. It's Our Lady. She goes everywhere with me. *(She smiles at him unkindly.)* And now thank you, Robert. Goodnight.
PLAYWRIGHT. Goodnight?
ACTRESS. I've booked another room for you.

PLAYWRIGHT. Another room? What do you mean "another room?"

ACTRESS. Another room! This is like your dialogue. Everything repeated. "Another room?" Yes. I've booked another room.

PLAYWRIGHT. What for?

ACTRESS. To sleep in

PLAYWRIGHT. What is this?

ACTRESS. What is it? It's me wanting to change.

PLAYWRIGHT. Change? Is this modesty? For God's sake you were in that play ...

ACTRESS. Don't talk about it.

PLAYWRIGHT. You were stark naked for an hour and a half. I personally saw the play three times.

ACTRESS. That's different. It's easier on stage.

(She goes behind a screen.)

PLAYWRIGHT. Perhaps I'll go for a walk. That always inspires me. I get all my best ideas at night. And knowing you're close, knowing my inspiration is near ...

ACTRESS. You do talk like a prick.

PLAYWRIGHT. Most women would say I talked ... like a poet.

ACTRESS. Yes, well. *(The ACTRESS has gotten into bed with a teddy.)* Now you can sit on the side of the bed and tell us a story.

PLAYWRIGHT. What sort of story do you want?

ACTRESS. Like ... who you're being unfaithful to right now?

PLAYWRIGHT. I'm not being unfaithful. Right now.

ACTRESS. I don't see why not. I am.

PLAYWRIGHT. Well that doesn't surprise me.

ACTRESS. And who do you think is the lucky man?

PLAYWRIGHT. I haven't the slightest idea.

ACTRESS. Guess.

PLAYWRIGHT. In the way of things, I suppose inevitably your producer.

ACTRESS. What do you think I am? Some sort of chorus girl?

PLAYWRIGHT. Sorry.

ACTRESS. Guess again.

PLAYWRIGHT. I don't know. The leading man. Benno.

ACTRESS. Benno? Do you know nothing. Benno lives with a postman.

PLAYWRIGHT. It's not possible.

ACTRESS. He's the most married man I've ever met. *(She smiles.)* Can I make a suggestion? Robert, just get into bed.

PLAYWRIGHT. That's what I wanted.

ACTRESS. And just get on with it.

PLAYWRIGHT. Well, that's what I've been saying! *(He is undressing quickly.)* Listen!

ACTRESS. What?

PLAYWRIGHT. The crickets are chirping

ACTRESS. Don't be ridiculous. There are no crickets round here.

PLAYWRIGHT. But you can hear them!

ACTRESS. Are we going to listen to nonexistent crickets all night? *(He gets into bed with her.)* Now just lie still.

PLAYWRIGHT. What are you doing?

ACTRESS. Can I ask you something? Are you thinking of having an affair with me.

PLAYWRIGHT. What on earth makes you think that.

ACTRESS. A lot of men want an affair with me.

PLAYWRIGHT. Yes, but right now, I'm in pole position.

ACTRESS. Come on then, cricket. From now on, I shall call you cricket.

PLAYWRIGHT. Cricket's good by me.

(She takes him in her arms.)

ACTRESS. Talk to me, come on, who do you think I'm betraying.

PLAYWRIGHT. It's a pretty good bet you're betraying me for a start.

ACTRESS. *(laughs.)* You're nuts.

PLAYWRIGHT. Somewhere perhaps there's a man you haven't met. A man who waits and is perfect.

ACTRESS. Cricket, you do talk bollocks.

PLAYWRIGHT. But if you met him, then you'd stop searching. And if you stopped searching ... well, if you stopped searching, then you wouldn't be you ...

(Darkness. Music engulfs them. The projected slide reads: TWENTY-FIVE MINUTES.)

• • • • •

(The music stops. Light comes up. They are lying, apparently exhausted, on the bed. A moment, then they start making love again. Darkness. Another projected slide reads: TWELVE MINUTES.)

• • • • •

(Light returns. They both look shattered.)

ACTRESS. Well you have to admit that's a lot better than acting in damn stupid plays.
PLAYWRIGHT. In my view, you act in rather good plays.
ACTRESS. Meaning yours?
PLAYWRIGHT. Well ...

(But she interrupts him, suddenly sincere.)

ACTRESS. I agree. Since you mention it. It is a great play.
PLAYWRIGHT. Thank you.
ACTRESS. You write brilliant plays.
PLAYWRIGHT. Thank you.

(There is a slight pause.)

ACTRESS. God sees what we do. I shall confess you tomorrow.

(He looks at her a moment, puzzled.)

PLAYWRIGHT. By the way, why did you skip that performance on Thursday? The doctor said you were fine.
ACTRESS. I did it to annoy you.
PLAYWRIGHT. Annoy me? Why?
ACTRESS. Because you're conceited.

PLAYWRIGHT. Me?

ACTRESS. You have no idea how everyone at the theatre hates you.

PLAYWRIGHT. They hate me?

ACTRESS. Of course! Behind your back. They all say you're conceited. I'm the only person who defends you. I tell them you've a lot to be conceited about.

PLAYWRIGHT. And what do they say to that?

ACTRESS. What do they say? What do they say? Who cares what the little people say?

PLAYWRIGHT. Well …

ACTRESS. You know what the theatre's like. A low drizzle of persistent complaint.

(The PLAYWRIGHT frowns, unhappy.)

PLAYWRIGHT. When you were saying … when you were saying about being a Catholic …

ACTRESS. Don't even speak of it. You can never understand. *(She nods.)* Yes, wild in the dark, and then the guilt.

PLAYWRIGHT. Even in love? Even when it's love?

ACTRESS. How often is it love?

PLAYWRIGHT. Fritz, I suppose.

ACTRESS. Fritz was special. You, you're a whim. *(She smiles, ignoring his hurt.)* Still suffering from the chirping are you?

PLAYWRIGHT. Non-stop. Can't you hear it?

ACTRESS. What you can hear is frogs, darling.

PLAYWRIGHT. Balls. Frogs croak.

ACTRESS. Well of course they *croak.*

PLAYWRIGHT. And that is not croaking, it's chirping.

ACTRESS. You are so bloody pigheaded. Give me a kiss, frog. *(They kiss.)* Happy now, frog. *(She laughs.)* Anyway, you've said nothing about my performance.

PLAYWRIGHT. When I heard you'd been off, I just assumed you'd be a bit creaky when you got back. So I didn't bother.

ACTRESS. Creaky? I was brilliant!

PLAYWRIGHT. Brilliant?

ACTRESS. People had to be carried out of the theatre.

PLAYWRIGHT. You saw them, did you? They had stretchers, did they?

ACTRESS. Benno said to me: "You act like an angel."

PLAYWRIGHT. Gosh! And fully recovered in twenty-four hours.

ACTRESS. You know nothing. The real reason I skipped the show was because I missed you so much!

PLAYWRIGHT. I thought you did it to annoy me.

ACTRESS. You're so fucking shallow, do you know that? I had a temperature of 105. All because of you.

PLAYWRIGHT. 105? That's quite a high temperature for a whim.

ACTRESS. A whim? I'm dying of love for you, and all you can call it is a whim.

(The PLAYWRIGHT smiles and takes her in his arms.)

PLAYWRIGHT. Are you acting? Just tell me, are you acting?

ACTRESS. Guess.

9. THE ACTRESS AND THE ARISTOCRAT

(The stage of the theatre, seen from the side. The sound of an ovation. The ACTRESS is dressed for a performance of a play by Schnitzler. She lifts her arms to thank her public, the curtain comes down and she turns towards us. Her dressing room is full of flowers. There is a period chaise-longue at one side of the room, and a table with some Chinese take-away on it. She goes out to the bathroom to start removing her costume. There is a nervous knock on the door and the ARISTOCRAT comes in, thin and exquisite, in his early 30s. The ACTRESS returns.)

ACTRESS. Good Lord ...
ARISTOCRAT. I'm sorry ...
ACTRESS. It's you.
ARISTOCRAT. The stage door-keeper suggested ...
ACTRESS. Please come in.
ARISTOCRAT. It never occurred to me ...
ACTRESS. Well I am.
ARISTOCRAT. That you wouldn't have changed.
ACTRESS. Sit down.

(He goes to perch nervously on the chaise-longue.*)*

ARISTOCRAT. You acted ...
ACTRESS. Thank you.
ARISTOCRAT. Like an angel.
ACTRESS. Is was something of a triumph, it seems.
ARISTOCRAT. *Something*? The audience were transported.
ACTRESS. Thank you for your flowers. *(She nods at the single huge bouquet of flowers.)* There they are.
ARISTOCRAT. Rather a small contribution, I'm afraid. You seem to be virtually buried by admirers.

(She looks at him a moment, then picks up all the flowers which are not his. She goes to the dressing room door, opens it, and throws them onto the floor in the corridor outside. She closes the door. Only his single vase of flowers remains.)

ACTRESS. There. That's better isn't it? *(She reaches for his hand impulsively and puts it to her lips.)* Don't worry. It commits you to nothing.

(He smiles.)

ARISTOCRAT. People warned me you were completely unpredictable. Some people say, an enigma.

ACTRESS. I'm certainly more of an enigma than your little Bridget Cluny.

ARISTOCRAT. Well there's very little mystery in Bridget. *(He quickly corrects himself.)* Not that she's someone I know all that well.

ACTRESS. No?

ARISTOCRAT. Do you know I had never seen you act until tonight?

ACTRESS. Incredible.

ARISTOCRAT. The theatre's a big problem for me. Parking! And then eating so late.

ACTRESS. Why not eat before?

ARISTOCRAT. Yes, I've considered that. I don't like restaurants much at the best of times.

ACTRESS. What do you like?

ARISTOCRAT. It's a good question.

ACTRESS. You seem to me something of a young fuddy-duddy.

(She goes out to the bathroom.)

ARISTOCRAT. Perhaps I just think too hard about things.

ACTRESS. *(off.)* Oh there's no point in thinking.

ARISTOCRAT. You're right. There is no point. People are people when it comes to it. I used to spend all my time thinking because

I was bored. I was farming the family estate. Though at least in the country there are horses. *(She returns. She is wrapping herself in a big dressing gown, letting him glimpse her whalebone corset.)* My God, why am I being so uninteresting?

ACTRESS. No, you're fascinating.

(He smiles at her.)

ARISTOCRAT. What about you? Are you fond of people?
ACTRESS. People? Lord, no. I can't stand them.
ARISTOCRAT. That's what I thought.
ACTRESS. I'm alone all the time. I'm virtually a recluse.
ARISTOCRAT. Of course.
ACTRESS. I see no one. No one!

(She has sat down at her dressing room table and is taking off her wig.)

ARISTOCRAT. But you're famous ... everywhere you go you're praised ...

ACTRESS. Praise? You think *praise* brings happiness? Please!

ARISTOCRAT. I didn't say happiness. That doesn't exist. Surely, isn't that what the play's saying?

ACTRESS. The play!

ARISTOCRAT. As I watched, I thought yes, this is true. This play says something true. When you fall in love, the feeling is there. It's real. It seems so real. Then, strange thing. It's gone.

ACTRESS. Malcolm, you go to the very heart of things.

(He shakes his head, thoughtfully.)

ARISTOCRAT. And so it scarcely matters, does it? Whether you're comfortable as I am, or mouse-poor. If you live in the town or in Timbuktu. For example ... I've lost my umbrella. Oh thank you ... now where was I?

ACTRESS. Timbuktu.

ARISTOCRAT. Oh yes. I'm rambling. But my life is a search.

ACTRESS. A search?
ARISTOCRAT. Yes. For a love which stays real

(She looks at him for a moment.)

ACTRESS. What are Miss Cluny's views on the subject?
ARISTOCRAT. What is this with Bridget?
ACTRESS. She is your girlfriend after all.
ARISTOCRAT. Is she?
ACTRESS. It says so in the papers.
ARISTOCRAT. Perhaps somebody should have told me.
ACTRESS. Oh Malcolm, come here! *(The ACTRESS laughs and pulls him towards her. She starts stroking his hair.)* I knew you were here tonight.
ARISTOCRAT. You knew? How?
ACTRESS. I spotted you.
ARISTOCRAT. What? From the stage?
ACTRESS. My whole performance was directed at you.
ARISTOCRAT. At me?
ACTRESS. Didn't you feel it? That diffidence of yours, your self-effacement …
ARISTOCRAT. I had no idea.
ACTRESS. It drives women nuts. And now kiss me at least … *(He leans across and kisses her.)* You are such a fake. Think how jealous every other man in the audience would be …
ARISTOCRAT. I know …
ACTRESS. Every night I feel them out there, pulsing, vibrating, like a physical force, all longing to rise up out of their seats, leap up on stage and have me on the boards …
ARISTOCRAT. Shall I tell you the truth? I'm frightened. *(He stops in agony.)* Let me explain. We've been frank with one another. I've reached a point in my life. I want things to be right. I want things to be perfect. The beginning has to be right. If I'm honest, what I want is not to do it right now. *(He pauses.)* And to be truthful, I find love not in a bed rather distasteful. *(He hastens to explain.)* With most — as it were — women, what does it matter? But with someone like you it's important. Because we will always remember

the first time. So ... please ...

ACTRESS. God, how adorable you are!

ARISTOCRAT. Let me tell you ...

ACTRESS. How sweet?

ARISTOCRAT. What I propose ...

ACTRESS. What do you propose?

ARISTOCRAT. Tomorrow, I collect you, we drive off, we book a hotel, somewhere out of town ...

ACTRESS. I am not Bridget Cluny!

ARISTOCRAT. I didn't say you were. I am saying: listen, romance is important. Mood is important. *(She has got up and locked the dressing room door. She turns off the lights.)* First, establish an atmosphere. And then ...

ACTRESS. Yes? Then?

ARISTOCRAT. Go on from there.

ACTRESS. A progress, you mean? A sequence?

ARISTOCRAT. There's a scent. What is it? A scent from the *chaise-longue.* Frangipani?

ACTRESS. It's so hot in here, don't you think?

(The ARISTOCRAT leans down and kisses her throat.)

ARISTOCRAT. Yes, it's hot.

ACTRESS. And dark, also, don't you think? Dark as night. *(She draws him closer.)* Oh Malcolm, are you sure? Is this the right start?

(Music engulfs them. Darkness. The projected slide reads: ONE HOUR ONE MINUTE.)

• • • • •

(The light returns. He is fully dressed, sitting at the little table using chopsticks on her cold Chinese take-away. She is lying back where we last saw her. They both look happy.)

ACTRESS. So?
ARISTOCRAT. Well?

(There is a silence. He eats.)

ACTRESS. What was that about *mood*?

ARISTOCRAT. Hmm …

ACTRESS. I thought *mood* was meant to be important. I thought not-in-a-bed was beneath you.

ARISTOCRAT. You're a bitch.

ACTRESS. Thank you.

ARISTOCRAT. Not a bitch. A goddess.

ACTRESS. And I think you were born to be an actor. Truly. You understand women completely.

(He stops eating a moment.)

ARISTOCRAT. Do you think any of us is ever just one person? Don't you think we all change, all the time? With one person we're one person, and with another we're another.

ACTRESS. You think so?

ARISTOCRAT. I do. I'm quite a different person when I'm mucking out.

(He looks at her, then resumes eating.)

ACTRESS. Do you know what I'm going to do now?

ARISTOCRAT. Do what?

ACTRESS. I'm going to tell you that I never want to see you ever again.

ARISTOCRAT. What are you saying?

ACTRESS. I'm out of my league. You're much too dangerous for me. You sit there as if nothing has happened. May I remind you: you've just debauched me.

ARISTOCRAT. *(smiles.)* Can I ever forget it?

ACTRESS. And tomorrow?

ARISTOCRAT. What tomorrow?

ACTRESS. Are you …

ARISTOCRAT. What, see you?

ACTRESS. Going to see me?

(Suddenly, he raises his voice, provoked by the inevitability of it all.)

ARISTOCRAT. What do we do? Tell me what we should do!

ACTRESS. What do you mean?

ARISTOCRAT. Don't we see already how this will unfold?

ACTRESS. No!

ARISTOCRAT. Don't we say "Oh yes! This is the moment when *this*!" and "Oh Lord! Here we go, here comes the moment when *that*!" Aren't we all stuck? Aren't we on a track? Aren't we welded to a track we can never get off? Don't we *know* already?

ACTRESS. Even if you were right, what's that? A reason for not doing anything? What are you saying? Nothing's worth doing because nothing ends well? *(He smiles, conceding.)* Philosophy? Thank you. I get it from a book.

ARISTOCRAT. Books teach us nothing.

ACTRESS. Well then there you are!

ARISTOCRAT. Nothing!

ACTRESS. You're right. Everything ends badly, because everyone dies! It's built into the story. Nobody escapes. So until then, what? This way, at least we're alive. We're alive! Meet me tomorrow. Learn. It's the only way of learning.

(They look at each other, in silence.)

ARISTOCRAT. I'll come to the theatre. I've stayed long enough. You have to act tomorrow.

ACTRESS. Not just tomorrow. Not just me.

(There is a silence. He takes the key from her. He goes to the door.)

ARISTOCRAT. Au revoir.

ACTRESS. Adieu, Timbuktu.

10. THE ARISTOCRAT AND THE GIRL

(At once the wail of a saxophone. Night streets, neon and alcohol. Dawn is breaking in a room above a sex shop in the center of the town. Outside it is raining and a red sign advertising the shop is seen through a thin film of curtain. Inside the room, the GIRL is asleep on the floor in her working clothes. On the other side of the room, the ARISTOCRAT is lying, fully dressed. Beside him there is a near-empty bottle of tequila. After a moment or two, the GIRL stirs and looks round, then goes back to sleep. A few moments later, the ARISTOCRAT wakes, obviously hungover and mystified by what he sees. He plainly has no memory of how he got here.)

ARISTOCRAT. Oh God, never again! I swore, never again! What did I do? Drink the whole day? *(He gets up, painfully. He rolls some words out to reassure himself he can speak.)* Amnesia. A medical term … for forgetting. *(He suddenly calls out in what seems like genuine despair.)* How do we change? How do we change who we are? *(The GIRL opens her eyes at the noise of his questions.)* Good morning.

GIRL. Hi, baby!

ARISTOCRAT. Did you sleep well?

GIRL. Mmm.

ARISTOCRAT. I was just off. *(She takes her hand out from under the blanket. She is tousled, warm. He shakes it, holding on a moment.)* As if she were divine!

GIRL. What are you staring at?

ARISTOCRAT. Oh, the way the light is falling. The way you woke. *(He looks at her a moment.)* How old are you?

GIRL. Twenty in December

ARISTOCRAT. And how long …

GIRL. A year.

ARISTOCRAT. A year. *(He takes out his wallet and removes a generous number of notes.)* I must go. *(She turns over to go back to sleep. He stops. Her face is turned towards him, the sun stronger now, as on a mask.)* May I ask you a favor? Please. Please don't say a word. *(He leans down and kisses her eyes.)* God, if you weren't … who you are, you could make your fortune.

GIRL. Yeah, that's what Fred says.

ARISTOCRAT. Fred? Who's Fred?

GIRL. Just a friend.

ARISTOCRAT. Oh yes? What does he do?

GIRL. He drives a cab.

ARISTOCRAT. I see. How did you meet him?

GIRL. Oh. By the river. A year ago.

ARISTOCRAT. You mean when you started? *(She does not answer.)* Are you close?

GIRL. He wants me to marry him.

ARISTOCRAT. That's nice. And what have you said?

GIRL. I'll only marry him if he lets me do something else.

ARISTOCRAT. And will he? Will Fred let you do something else? *(She does not answer. He makes to go.)* Perhaps we'll meet again.

(The GIRL's eyes remain closed.)

GIRL. Just ask for Irene.

ARISTOCRAT. Irene. Fair enough. *(He stops once more at the door.)* Still, it's something, eh? I've spent the whole night with her and all I've done is kiss her eyes. That's something. *(He smiles, pleased with himself.)* Irene, does this happen a lot?

GIRL. What?

ARISTOCRAT. That men leave you. That they just leave you?

GIRL. Sure, every day.

ARISTOCRAT. No, I mean without … without …

GIRL. No. Never!

ARISTOCRAT. It doesn't mean I don't like you.

GIRL. I know that. You liked me well enough last night.

(The ARISTOCRAT frowns.)

ARISTOCRAT. I like you now.

GIRL. Yet, but you liked me better last night. *(The light is growing at the window, circling her with yellow.)* Don't tell me you've forgotten.

ARISTOCRAT. Yes. No.

GIRL. Then afterwards you fell asleep.

ARISTOCRAT. Yes. I do that. That's what I did, then.

(There is a silence. She is quite still and her tone is kind.)

GIRL. God, you must have been drunk, baby.

ARISTOCRAT. Yes. *(The GIRL gets up to join him at the window.)* Well ... it would have been romantic if I'd just kissed your eyes. That would have been romantic. It would have been ... pure. But there we are. It wasn't to be.

GIRL. On we go.

ARISTOCRAT. Yes, on we go. *(In the distance, the day is starting. The town is coming to life and the saxophone is beginning to play again. The GIRL stands up and sleepily drags her bed across the room. They look at one another for a moment.)* Good night.

GIRL. Good morning.

ARISTOCRAT. Yes of course. Good morning. Good morning.

(The music grows louder. He stands, not moving. Then he turns decisively and goes. The GIRL goes out to the riverside where she stands a moment, waiting for trade. She lifts her arm to a man we do not see.)

GIRL. Hey!

TREASURE ISLAND
Ken Ludwig

All Groups / Adventure / 10m, 1f (doubling) / Areas

Based on the masterful adventure novel by Robert Louis Stevenson, *Treasure Island* is a stunning yarn of piracy on the tropical seas. It begins at an inn on the Devon coast of England in 1775 and quickly becomes an unforgettable tale of treachery and mayhem featuring a host of legendary swashbucklers including the dangerous Billy Bones (played unforgettably in the movies by Lionel Barrymore), the sinister two-timing Israel Hands, the brassy woman pirate Anne Bonney, and the hideous form of evil incarnate, Blind Pew. At the center of it all are Jim Hawkins, a 14-year-old boy who longs for adventure, and the infamous Long John Silver, who is a complex study of good and evil, perhaps the most famous hero-villain of all time. Silver is an unscrupulous buccaneer-rogue whose greedy quest for gold, coupled with his affection for Jim, cannot help but win the heart of every soul who has ever longed for romance, treasure and adventure.

THE OFFICE PLAYS
Two full length plays by Adam Bock

THE RECEPTIONIST
Comedy / 2m., 2f. Interior

At the start of a typical day in the Northeast Office, Beverly deals effortlessly with ringing phones and her colleague's romantic troubles. But the appearance of a charming rep from the Central Office disrupts the friendly routine. And as the true nature of the company's business becomes apparent, The Receptionist raises disquieting, provocative questions about the consequences of complicity with evil.

"...Mr. Bock's poisoned Post-it note of a play."
- New York Times

"Bock's intense initial focus on the routine goes to the heart of *The Receptionist's* pointed, painfully timely allegory... elliptical, provocative play..."
- Time Out New York

THE THUGS
Comedy / 2m, 6f / Interior

The Obie Award winning dark comedy about work, thunder and the mysterious things that are happening on the 9th floor of a big law firm. When a group of temps try to discover the secrets that lurk in the hidden crevices of their workplace, they realize they would rather believe in gossip and rumors than face dangerous realities.

"Bock starts you off giggling, but leaves you with a chill."
- Time Out New York

"... a delightfully paranoid little nightmare that is both more chillingly realistic and pointedly absurd than anything John Grisham ever dreamed up."
- New York Times

A VERY MERRY UNAUTHORIZED CHILDREN'S SCIENTOLOGY PAGEANT

Kyle Jarrow

Musical / 5m, 5f (Doubling possible) / Interior

A jubilant cast of children celebrate the controversial religion in uplifting pageantry and song. The actual teachings of The Church of Scientology are explained and dissected against the candy-colored backdrop of a traditional nativity play. Pageant is a musical biography of the life of L. Ron Hubbard, with child-friendly explanations of Hubbard's notion of the divided mind (embodied by the lovely identical twins Emma and Sophie Whitfield in matching brain outfits) and a device called the e-meter (or electropsychometer), used to monitor the human psyche, which is demonstrated by stick puppets. Grade school children, portraying Tom Cruise, Kirstie Alley, John Travolta, and other less starry Scientologists, brings the controversial Church of Scientology to jubilant life in story and song.

ELECTION DAY
Josh Tobiessen

Full Length / Comedy / 2m, 2f / Unit Set

It's Election Day, and Adam knows his over-zealous girlfriend will never forgive him if he fails to vote. But when his sex starved sister, an eco-terrorist, and a mayoral candidate willing to do anything for a vote all show up, Adam finds that making that quick trip to the polls might be harder than he thought. *Election Day* is a hilarious dark comedy about the price of political (and personal) campaigns.

"An outrageous comedy… at double-espresso speed."
- The New York Times

"Ridiculously entertaining… cute and cutting."
- Variety

"Laugh-out-loud."
- Backstage

"Delightfully farcical… Tobiessen takes a simple premise and spins it out into a hilarious sequence of events. His dialogue is lean and playful, and includes some terrific lines."
- Theatermania

BACH AT LEIPZIG
Itamar Moses

Comedy Farce / 7m / Interior

Leipzig, Germany — 1722. Johann Kuhnau, revered organist of the Thomaskirche, suddenly dies, leaving his post vacant. The town council invites musicians from across to audition for the coveted position, among them young Johann Sebastian Bach. In an age where musicians depend on patronage from the nobility or the church to pursue their craft, the post at a prominent church in a cultured city is a near guarantee of fame and fortune – which is why some of the candidates are willing to resort to any lengths to secure it. *Bach at Leipzig* is a fugue-like farcical web of bribery, blackmail, and betrayal set against the backdrop of Enlightenment questions about humanity, God, and art.